This Notebook Belongs To

Made in the USA
Las Vegas, NV
29 December 2022

64405806R00070